The Kids Guide to Money Cent$

Written by **Keltie Thomas**

Illustrated by **Stephen MacEachern**

Kids Can Press

For big spenders, Trader Js and penny pinchers everywhere — K.T.
To Jeanette, you are priceless — S.M.

Acknowledgments

Many thanks to all the wonderful people at Kids Can Press, especially Stephen MacEachern,
Liz MacLeod and Julia Naimska.

Special thanks to Paul S. Berry, Chief Curator of the National Currency Collection, Bank of Canada;
Laurie Campbell and Fergus T. Millar, Credit Counselling of Toronto; Richard Doty, Smithsonian National
Museum of American History; Devon Green, Devon's Heal the World Recycling; Ryan Hreljac, Ryan's
Well Foundation; Jennifer Kellogg, Director of Education at Consumer Credit Counseling Service of
Olympic-South Sound, Tacoma, Washington; Chloe MacBeth, T.L.C. Kennels; Cohen MacInnis, Happyface
Printing & Publishing; Elise Macmillan, The Chocolate Farm; John J. Norman, Phillips, Hager & North
Investment Management Ltd.; and PJ.

Text © 2004 Keltie Thomas
Illustrations © 2004 Stephen MacEachern

Kids Can Press acknowledges the financial support of the Government of Ontario, through the Ontario
Media Development Corporation's Ontario Book Initiative; the Ontario Arts Council; the Canada
Council for the Arts; and the Government of Canada, through the BPIDP, for our publishing activity.

Kids Can Press Ltd.
2250 Military Road
Tonawanda, NY 14150

www.kidscanpress.com

Edited by Elizabeth MacLeod
Designed by Julia Naimska
Printed and bound in China

The hardcover edition of this book is smyth sewn casebound.
The paperback edition of this book is limp sewn with a drawn-on-cover.

US 04 0 9 8 7 6 5 4 3 2 1
US PA 04 0 9 8 7 6 5 4

National Library of Canada Cataloguing in Publication Data

Thomas, Keltie
        The kids guide to money cent$ / written by Keltie Thomas ; illustrated by Stephen MacEachern.

Includes index.
ISBN 978-1-55337-389-6 (bound)
ISBN 978-1-55337-390-2 (pbk.)

1. Finance, Personal — Juvenile literature. 2. Money — Juvenile literature.

3. Children — Finance, Personal — Juvenile literature.
I. MacEachern, Stephen II. Title.

HG179.T52 2004   j332.024'054   C2003-903677-4

Kids Can Press is a *Corus*™ Entertainment company

Contents

Money Cent$ Gang

Ask Alicia, Dan and Jeff how the Money Cent$ Gang was born and you'll get three different answers.

"All right, all right! It did start with me," says Dan. "Talk about being in the hole. Just thinking about it makes my cheeks burn! Practically the whole school was there watching the game when we won the Midtown junior baseball championships. The score was tied at the bottom of the ninth. Bases were loaded and we had two outs when we got a home run. Yess!

"And that's when I blew it. I hit the ice-cream truck to celebrate. 'Cones for all my teammates,' I said. When the server handed me the last one with 'That'll be $26.75, sir,' I said, 'No problem.' I reached into my pocket and pulled out a $20 bill, then fished around for some more dough and came up empty-handed."

"Then you checked every single one of your other pockets," notes Alicia.

"It was an ugly scene, all right," adds Jeff.

"Thanks for reminding me." Dan rolls his eyes. "Anyhow, the $20 was all I had. I'd raided my piggy bank that morning for the big day and left the house flush — with thirty bucks and change jingling in my pocket.

"So I held out the $20. 'Uh, it's all I've got left … I was sure I had more, but …' Luckily, the coach came to the rescue and plunked down another $20. Phew!"

I can't believe you didn't try to cut a deal, like washing dishes — or something.

What dishes? They were ice-cream cones.

"Unluckily for Jeff and me, Coach Richter is also our social studies teacher," points out Alicia.

"Right, I was getting to that part," says Danny. "The next day in class, Mr. Richter gave the three of us the topic of money for our research project. 'It's time you kids made some sense of dollars and cents,' he said. The whole class roared and I turned beet red."

"Needless to say," Danny continues, "Alicia was less than impressed. 'Look what you've gotten us into now, Spendy Boy,' she groaned. But Jeff turned to the class and said, 'Just call us the Money Cent$ Gang. We're going to get the inside scoop on money and how to make it, earn it, spend it, save it — you name it. Joining our gang costs only a buck.' After that, our name kind of stuck."

Never mind the buck. Just turn the page and join us as we get the lowdown on dough for our project.

What Is Money?

Today we're going to explore the origins of money. Quick — what's money? Say the first thing that comes into your mind.

Stuff you buy stuff with.

Uh, bills and coins.

Something I could use more of!

I was right!

Money Is ...

... something we all agree on.

When you get right down to it, money is just a bunch of coins and bills — bits of metal and pieces of paper. What makes these bits and pieces valuable is the fact that we all agree on what each one is worth.

For example, while a $10 bill is made of the same stuff as a $5 bill and is exactly the same size and weight, we all agree the $10 bill is worth twice as much. Even though these values may be in our heads, they make money very powerful.

Money's mind-blowing stuff!

... what we use to buy stuff.

Since everyone agrees on the value of money, you can use it to buy practically anything you want: burgers and fries, sneakers, snowboards — even the roof over your family's head!

Businesses exchange things and services for money because of its value. Then they can turn around and use it to buy things, too. Money is a means of exchange that allows people to get exactly what they need and want. Or they can save it and use it in the future.

... not something that grows on trees!

Every country decides what kind of money it will use. But that doesn't mean countries can make as much cash as they like. First, the more money a country makes, the more money that is available and the less it is worth.

Second, the more money that's available, the more products people buy. And the more products people buy, the fewer that are available. So prices go up, and people can't buy as much with their money. Then the country has to make more money, and so on and so on.

Sometimes this can make prices rise out of control. After World War I, for example, Germany printed loads of cash to pay its war debts. A loaf of bread soon cost a wheelbarrow full of German cash! Germany had to print money so fast that it had time to print only one side of the bills.

Workers were paid cash daily and were given so many bills that they had to carry their pay home in boxes, laundry bags or wheelbarrows. If they didn't spend their money that night, prices rose so much the money was almost worthless the next day.

The Life and Times of Money

Your average bill jumps off the printing press crisp, clean and ready for action! It's made of seventy-five per cent cotton and twenty-five per cent linen to stand up to the wear and tear of constant handling. You can fold it forwards then backwards thousands of times before it will tear!

Even so, the average $1 bill lasts just twenty-two months before it's dirty and worn out. Once old bills end up at the bank, they're replaced by new bills, shredded and recycled to make greeting cards, roof shingles and wallpaper.

Why We Need Money

Go Money-Free and See

Living in a world without money isn't easy. Trading for things, or bartering, as people did long ago before money existed, is anything but simple. For starters, you have to find someone who has what you want and is willing to trade it for something that you've got and you're willing to trade. Then you both have to agree it's a trade of equal value. It's a good bet ancient people got so fed up with bartering that they invented money.

World's Biggest Barter Bargain?

Today, the island of Manhattan is the heart of New York City. But chances are, not much was there in 1626. That's when Native American chiefs bartered the island to a Dutch man for some jewelry and trinkets worth $24. Talk about a steal of a deal!

LUNCHTIME BARTER BOGGLE

Can you use the trade rates and clues below to help Jeff barter his salmon sandwich for Josie's pizza slice in as few trades as possible?

(See the answer on page 56.)

Trade rates
pizza slice = peanut butter and jelly sandwich
    = chocolate bar = burrito and 2 Oreo cookies
Oreo cookie = 5 jelly beans
chocolate bar = 4 Oreos
salmon sandwich = burrito

Clues
1. Neither Josie nor Khadija will eat salmon.
2. Raoul says his chocolate bar is not for sale, er, trade.
3. Josie will trade for the chocolate bar but not the peanut butter and jelly sandwich.

Jeff's lunch: salmon sandwich, fruit cup, 20 jelly beans
Josie's lunch: all-dressed pizza slice, apple
Raoul's lunch: beef burrito, chocolate bar
Khadija's lunch: peanut butter and jelly sandwich, 8 carrot sticks, 5 Oreos

That's Dough? Whoa!

Cows: In ancient Egypt, cows were exchanged just like money, er, moolah!

Stone "doughnuts": Around 1900, people on Yap Island in the Pacific Ocean used giant stones with a hole in the middle as money. Some stones were as heavy as a small car!

Salt: Long ago, Roman soldiers were given a lump of salt for their wages. In fact, the word "salary" comes from this custom.

Your Money Personality

What's Your Money Personality?

Does money slip through your fingers or pile up in your piggy bank? In an ongoing Web survey, here's what kids aged five to sixteen who get an allowance had to say:

- **22 per cent save it up to buy something special**
- **17 per cent spend half and save the rest**
- **15 per cent spend it all right away**
- **12 per cent spend most and save the rest**
- **5 per cent save it for emergencies**
- **2 per cent don't know what they usually do with their allowance**

How cents-ible or cents-less are you with your dough? Take this quiz to find out.

1. What's your "money attitude"?
a) Money grows on trees — I just haven't figured out which ones yet
b) I need money to survive, but money can't buy me love
c) A penny saved is a penny earned

2. Your dough usually
a) Goes in one pocket and out the other
b) Gets split between your pockets and your piggy bank
c) All goes into your piggy bank

3. If you won a million dollars, you'd
a) Throw a big party and spend it all on cool stuff for you and your friends and family
b) Jump up and down — Wahoo! — then spend some and save some
c) Stash ninety-nine per cent of it away for a rainy day and/or a college education

4. Your friends call you
a) Moneybags, and aren't shy to ask you to "spot" them in a "pinch"
b) The Cents-ible One, and ask you how you always stay "in the money"
c) Tightwad, but only when they think you can't hear

5. When it comes to IOUs
a) You rack them up against your next allowance or paycheck
b) You rarely need them but are willing to give them
c) You wouldn't be caught dead asking for one or giving one

When you've finished the quiz, count how many A answers you chose, B answers and C answers. See how you rate on page 56.

Your Cash Flow?

Does Your Cash Flow In or Out?

You don't need to be a math whiz to figure out your cash flow.

Your cash flow = **Incoming cash** − **Outgoing cash**
(regular cash sources: allowance, birthday gifts, pay from a job) (regular expenses: bus fare, lunch, snacks, anything you spend money on)

First, add up all your incoming cash. Then add up all your outgoing cash and subtract this number from your incoming cash. Now you've got your cash flow — the money you have available to do whatever you want — donate, save, spend …

DEAR DIARY, WHY AM I ALWAYS BROKE?

Where, oh where, does your money go? To find out, keep a money diary for a week. Carry a pen and paper with you at all times and write down every cent you spend and what you spend it on. Check out Danny's diary.

DANNY'S MONEY DIARY

Monday	Tuesday	Wednesday	Thursday	Friday (Allowance Day)	Saturday	Sunday
Bus tickets $7.50 Good luck four-leaf clover tattoos for team (12 @ 25¢ ea.) $3 Arcade games $2	Forgot bus ticket, had to pay fare $1 Chocolate bar $1.50 Arcade games $2	Searched everywhere — no cash	Arcade games $3 — IOU to Jeff	Pop $1 Lost track of how many arcade games played. Think I spent $10.	Arcade games $5 Lunch at Burger Palace $3.50	Movie ticket $5 Popcorn $3 Bubblegum for me, Jeff, Alicia 3¢
Total: $12.50	Total: $4.50	Total: $0	Total: $3	Total: $11	Total: $8.50	Total: $8.03

The Cost of Living?!

Face it: living in today's world costs money. You and your family have to shell out for clothes, food, the roof over your heads and more. These are your costs of living. And they vary depending on where you live.

The government keeps an eye on the prices of hundreds of products and services across the country — clothes, food, furniture, haircuts, housing, medical fees, transportation — because they affect how well you live. For example, if prices rise, your cost of living goes up. You must spend more just to survive, so your cash flow goes down. Then you have less money to spend, or disposable income.

On the other hand, if prices fall, your cost of living goes down. And your cash flow goes up! The government tries to keep the cost of living stable so people can afford all the things they need — and more.

Lish even made me write down the 3¢ for bubblegum.

That's the whole point of the diary, Dough Head!

Saving Your Cash

Saving Adds Up

Saving makes cents — in more ways than one. And kids know it. When *Zillions*, the magazine for kids published by *Consumer Reports*, asked kids what New Year's resolutions they had made, the top one was "Save or make money." If you save

- you won't go broke
- you can buy the things you want, not just the things your parents say you need
- you'll have an emergency stash if unexpected expenses pop up
- you can share your money with those less fortunate than you

You may even find that you enjoy spending your money more. Go figure!

> Even though she doesn't like to admit it, Alicia really is a fab saver.

> So Danny and I convinced her to give us some tips.

> I picked my Gran's brain for her two cents worth, too.

Alicia's Money-Savers

- Save up for something you really, really want — you're more likely to save.
- Don't carry around all your cash. That way, you can't blow it all.
- Every time some cash comes your way, tuck some of it away — right away.
- Don't try to save every penny. Save some and spend some.
- Stash your cash in the bank, so it's out of your hands.

Not Everything Costs Money

What's the number one thing you spend money on? Having fun? Who says you need money to have fun? Hanging out with friends is free and so is telling jokes and having a laugh.

You can also find lots of free stuff that usually comes with a price tag: baseball caps, food and drink samples, movie passes, pens, posters, stickers, tote bags, toys, T-shirts … Keep your eyes peeled for freebies during special events at festivals, malls, museums, sports games or stores.

> Freebies — my fave!

Budgeting for Goals

With a Budget, You Rule!

While you may not be able to control how much cash you have coming in, you can control where it goes once it's in your hands. How? With a budget! Making a budget is the number one thing you can do to get the most out of money. Try it and see.

1. Figure out your cash flow on page 12.

2. Is your cash flow more than zero? Great, you've got money to save. If not, go back to step 1 and cut out some of your regular expenses until it is.

3. Find ways to save. Look at your expenses (outgoing cash) and sort them into

   NEEDS   **WANTS**
   things you cannot do without   things you can do without

   Now look at your WANTS. What can you cut back on or cut out altogether so you'll have more money to save for stuff you really want? Figure out your new cash flow — how much you can save each week or month.
   The idea is to cut out stuff that's not important to get the stuff that is important. Cool!

4. Make a list of the stuff you really want to save for. Put them in order from most to least wanted.

5. Make a plan to get the first goal on your list.
   Plan for reaching goal #1: PlayRation game ($90)
   Savings per week: $5
   Birthday money on May 16: $50
   Price – Birthday money = Money still needed
   $90 – $50 = $40
   Money still needed ÷ Savings per week = # of weeks to save
   $40 ÷ $5 = 8 weeks to save

6. Carry out your plan. Save money until you have enough for your first goal. Buy it and celebrate! Then start saving toward your next goal.

> Danny Boy, you're ahead of the game. You've already done step 1.

> Stuff I want: PlayRation game, new bike, backpack …

What's It Worth?

Danny and the Arcade: To Play or Not to Play?

Hey, Arcade Boy! Reality's tough!

My saving goal: I really want a new BMX bike to ride in the King of Dirt competition this summer. My old bike's getting too small for me.

My temptations: I love going to arcades. Where else can you race Formula Ones and go skydiving — virtually? But playing games could really bust my budget.

My budget: When I did my money diary, I found out that playing arcade games is where most of my money goes. If I keep playing four or five days a week, I'll never be able to save up enough for the bike. That would really stink.

What gives: If I hit the arcade only on Saturdays, I can save what I need. I'm going to tell Jeff and Alicia so they can help me stick to it.

Alicia's Dilemma: Logo or No Go?

My saving goal: When I got my new board, I started saving for some cool skater gear right away. Lucky for me, I didn't have to save long because everybody gave me money for my birthday.

My temptations: I can buy the top and shorts today. Yess! But I just heard that tickets for the X-Dudes concert go on sale tomorrow. And I really want to go!

My budget: Tickets are $50, and the skater gear is $160 — ouch! But I've shopped around and that's the best price. What I'm really paying for is the tiny logo on the gear! I saw a top and shorts that were practically identical for about half the price.

What gives: That's it! I'll buy the clothes without the logos. Then I'll be able to go to the concert and even have some money left over. That's totally worth it!

Whoa! Are logos worth that much?

The Most Expensive Sneakers on Earth?

Experts say the more rare something is, the more it's worth. But sometimes the value of something all comes down to how much someone is willing to pay for it.

In 1985, a pair of Air Jordan sneakers (named for basketball superstar Michael Jordan), found unused in their box, went for $3000.

Maybe you need to think about your options.

Jeff's Quest: Digital Camera or Bust!

My saving goal: My dad's old camera is great. But with a digital cam, I could upload shots to my Web site right away: Jeff's eye on the world coming at ya! With all this saving and budgeting, I figure there's got to be a way to afford it.

My temptations: CD burner, cell phone, comics, cool shades, hockey cards …

My budget: It doesn't cost anything to wish for cool stuff, right? My main problem is zilch in the incoming cash department: no regular allowance, no job. I could sell my hockey cards for cash. But I just traded for the top card in the book — the Wayne Gretzky rookie card. And I bet my collection's going to be worth a lot someday. There's got to be another way …

What gives: The camera shop sells used stuff. That's my option! I can trade in my dad's old camera, then buy a used digital cam for way less than a new one.

Is It Really Worth It?

So you've got cash to drop on the latest pair of "cool brand" jeans or sneakers or the hottest CD. Before you step into the store, ask yourself these questions to figure out if you really have to blow your bucks:

1. Do I really need <u>the latest pair of "cool brand" jeans?</u> Now, ask yourself this question again, but leave the brand name out.
2. How many other <u>pairs of jeans</u> do I have?
3. How much will I use <u>the jeans?</u>
4. Will I still want <u>the jeans</u> this much in two weeks? A month? Six months?
5. If I buy <u>the jeans</u>, how far will it set me back from getting what I really want?

Are You an Ad Target?

You bet you are. Advertisers beam TV ads at you at home and at school, banner ads while you're surfing the Net and billboard ads as you walk down the street. They plaster logos on your clothes and schoolbooks, and they even slip their products into the movies you watch!

Why are advertisers working overtime to get your attention? According to a 1998 *Consumer Reports* study, you and other US kids have a combined total of $15 billion of your own money to spend each year. What's more, you have influence where it counts — on your parents' wallets. Studies show that American kids "nag" their parents into buying stuff to the tune of $188 billion a year.

Buy Nothing Day

Do not shop. Do not buy a single thing for twenty-four hours! That's the name of the game on Buy Nothing Day — the last Friday of November. The idea's caught on in many countries around the world. Buy Nothing Day is a chance to take a break from shopping and think about what you buy and why.

Sometimes, people buy products they don't need because ads for them make people think the products will make their lives better. Or ads make people feel as if they're losers if they don't have the stuff. So they buy it — only to find that their lives remain exactly the same!

On Buy Nothing Day, people don't buy anything, so they can instead think about what they really want out of life — things money can't buy. Best of all, it's absolutely free!

2 ¢ WORTH
Did you know the average twelve-year-old watches the tube for four hours a day? That means she's bombarded by 20 000 to 40 000 TV ads a year!

Shopping Around

Shopping around Makes Cents

Prices often vary from store to store, brand to brand and model to model. So shopping around can really pay off. Follow these shopping tips to help get the most bang for your buck:

- If you know exactly what you want, call to find out which stores carry it and compare prices. Ask if it will be going on sale soon.
- Check out different brands. Can you find one that meets all your needs and costs less than the others? Do any friends have that brand? What do they think of its performance?
- Check out different models and compare prices. Do you really need all the features a particular model has? Can you do what you want with fewer features and save yourself some money?
- Always keep your eyes peeled for sales on what you're looking for.

The Case of Danny and His Dream Bike

Okay, maybe I hadn't shopped around "exactly." But that doesn't mean I was about to get hosed. When I decided to compete in the BMX circuit this summer, I knew I needed a lean, mean machine that was up to the challenge. Oh yeah, and one that wouldn't break the bank. So I went online and researched brands and models.

Then I hit the bike shop and test-rode my faves. The BMX 500 came out on top. It has the same lightweight frame as pro bikes. It's really fast and it gets good height on jumps, which just might be the winning edge I need. But it isn't made for the pros, so it sells for much less. You know what? Once I told Alicia and Jeff all that, I think they were impressed!

Wow, Dan! You really did your homework.

Make that shopwork!

Buyer Beware

Don't Get Scammed

Most people think it will never happen to them. But anyone can get scammed. Remember: if a deal looks too good to be true, it probably is! Use this checklist to help make sure you don't get ripped off:

- Is the product made by a well-known company? Does it come with a money-back guarantee or warranty that the company will repair or replace defects without charge? What does the warranty cover and how long does it last?
- Do you know anyone who has the product? If so, would they buy it again?
- Is it on sale for an unbelievably low price? If so, ask the seller how he can afford to sell the product for so little. Is a new or better model about to come out, for example?
- What's the return policy? Will the seller refund your money or only exchange the product? Is the return policy the same for sale items?
- Always keep your receipt for returns and as proof of purchase.
- Check for "hidden costs," such as assembly or installation charges, batteries, delivery or shipping fees or sales tax. Then you'll know the product's real cost before you buy it.

I never thought it could happen to me!

Watch Out for Sales Gimmicks

Red tag sales: When stores want to clear unsold products off their shelves, they often discount them and attach red tags to show the "incredible" savings. That way, you may buy something just because it's a good "deal," even if you don't need it.

Eye level: Some stores stock expensive name brands at eye level — right where you're most likely to look — and less expensive brands higher up or lower down on their shelves. When you shop around, be sure to look around, too!

Hero endorsements: Is your favorite athlete or celebrity hawking sneakers or pop on a poster? Hero endorsements like these try to convince you that if you buy the product, you will be just as popular as your hero shown using it.

Banks

Just How Safe Are Banks?

Very! Banks are about the safest places on Earth to put your money. First, banks store money in fireproof vaults that have high-tech locks and alarms designed to keep out even the cash-hungriest of criminals.

Second, the government, or the Federal Deposit Insurance Corporation (FDIC) to be exact, guarantees up to $100 000 of your money that's deposited in an FDIC-insured bank. So even if robbers steal all the cash or if the bank goes broke, you don't have to panic. The FDIC will pay back up to $100 000 of your dough. Phew!

Talking 'bout Banks

Bank — Comes from the Italian word *banca*, which means "bench." In the Middle Ages, Italian moneylenders sat on benches in the market to do business.

Bankable — Means "reliable" or "sure to make money."

Bank on it — Means "rely on it." This saying is based on people's trust in banks to keep their money safe.

Bankrupt — Comes from the Italian words for "broken bench," *banca rotta*.

Piggy banks — Long ago, people stashed extra cash in pots and jugs made of pygg clay and called them pygg banks or pyggy banks. One day, someone made a pot in the shape of a pig and the term "piggy bank" was coined.

How banks make money, right this way!

Banks Pay You!

Hot on the Money Trail

What happens when you deposit your hard-earned cash in a bank? It puts your money to work — to make more money!

The bank loans your money to local people and businesses. (Putting your bucks in the bank helps make money available to your community.) The bank charges them a fee for the loans, called interest. This gives the bank money to pay you an interest fee for keeping your money at the bank.

Because the interest the bank pays you is less than the interest it charges on loans, the bank makes a profit. And it makes sure it always has enough cash on hand so you can take out your money whenever you want.

Money Grows on Interest

Sound far-fetched? Say you deposit $100 in an account that pays ten per cent interest per year. At the end of a year, you'd have $100 plus $10 of interest, for a total of $110. During the next year, you'd earn compound interest — interest on your original deposit plus the added interest. At the end of that year, you'd have $110 plus $11 of compound interest — $121.

If you left the money in the account to keep earning compound interest, you'd double your money for a total of $200 in 7.2 years — without adding a penny more! That's how money grows on interest.

Hidden Costs of Banking

Sure banks pay you for putting your money in them. But they also make you pay to take your money out! Banks charge withdrawal fees when you withdraw money. They charge checking fees when you write checks — instructions to the bank to pay a sum of money from your account to a certain person or company. They also charge fees when you pay for things with a debit card, which automatically withdraws the money from your account.

It's important to shop around for an account with low service fees. And find out whether you'll be hit with a fee if your account dips below a "minimum balance." Ask for a brochure about how the account works. Then read the fine print so you know all the ins and outs of your money going in and out.

The Rule of Seventy-Two and You

How long would it take you to double your savings through compound interest without adding another cent? Just plug your interest rate into "the Rule of Seventy-Two."

72 ÷ interest rate = # of years to double your money*

*Interest rates change constantly. As they change, so does the number of years it takes to double your money.

Fantastic Plastic

The Inside Scoop

Credit allows you to buy something now and pay for it later. The world's first multipurpose credit card charged on the scene in 1950. One day Francis Xavier McNamara took some clients to a fancy restaurant for lunch. When the waiter presented the bill, Francis discovered that he had left all his cash at home!

Francis vowed never to be caught short of cash again. He invented the Diner's Club card, which people could use for drinks, entertainment, meals and travel, then pay the bill a month later.

The Catch: Interesting Fees ...

Today, you can use plastic credit cards to buy almost anything anywhere you go. When the monthly bill arrives, you can pay off the total of your purchases or a "minimum monthly payment." Pay the total and you won't pay any interest (a fee on top of your purchases). But pay the minimum monthly payment, or any less than the total, and the card company will zing you for interest on the rest.

Over time, interest fees can even double the price of your purchases. So when you pay by credit card, remember: sooner or later, you have to pay it all back — and even more if it's later!

Charging Yourself to Debt

Credit cards allow people to buy what they want even if they haven't first saved all of the money to pay for it. But this makes it easy to spend money they don't have. When people use plastic instead of cash, they often don't think about how much they're spending! Many fall deeply into debt, struggling to pay their credit card bills.

Got to Give Him Credit

Walter Cavanagh just can't get enough credit. According to Guinness World Records, the credit card collector from Santa Clara, California, has the most credit cards in the world — 1397. If he stacked them end to end, they'd reach the top of a four-story building.

Each of Walter's cards is different, and he keeps them in the world's longest wallet, which is 250 ft. long. But Walter knows how to handle credit without sinking into debt. He uses only two or three cards and pays off his bills every month.

Making Money

Cool Jobs for Kids

Wanted:
Kid Actor

Play the part of a kid in movies, on TV shows or in commercials. It's a job only a kid can do!

What it takes:
- A thick skin: Actors try out, or audition, for many parts and often get rejected.
- Flexible parents: Auditions, rehearsals and filming often happen during school. You'll need your parents' permission to catch up on your studies later.

What you make:
- Anywhere from $0 to $$$. It all depends on what roles and how many you get.

Is it for you?*
- Do you enjoy being in the spotlight?
- Can you work on your own to catch up on schoolwork you miss?

Wanted:
Friendly Dog Walker

Looking for a new leash on life? Escort Fido and Rover on their daily excursions.

What it takes:
- Love at pooch sight: Do you love dogs? Are you comfortable meeting strange dogs?
- Patience: Canines are curious. Sometimes it may seem as if they have to sniff every rock and tree before they get down to business and pee.

What you make:
- Around $4 per hour, depending on where you live.

Is it for you?*
- Do you have time to walk dogs twice a day?
- Can you scoop poop without losing your cookies?

*If you answer no to any of these questions, the job's probably not for you. Sorry!

More Cool Jobs for Kids

Bait-worm wrangler, bike repair dude, car washer, computer tutor, dog washer and groomer, errand runner, gardener, gift shopper, house-sitter, jewelry maker, parent helper, party clown, party planner, pet photographer, pet-sitter

Talk seriously so people take you seriously.

Wanted:
Human Lawn Mowing Machine

Kids often get regular grass cutting gigs. Several jobs may be growing right under your nose!

What it takes:
- Tool know-how: You need to know how to operate a lawn mower and/or a trimmer. Don't use any equipment or tools that are unfamiliar to you.
- Attention to detail: Homeowners may ask you to cut in a certain direction, rake up clippings or avoid areas where grass seed or fertilizer has been put down.

What you make:
- Around $5 per hour, depending on where you live.

Is it for you? *
- Can you remember the details the customer asks for?
- Can you get the job done even if your friends are playing nearby in the sun?

Help! How Do I Get a Job?

Just follow these four steps:

1. Put the word out: Tell everybody you know you're looking for a job. Sound crazy? Many jobs are never advertised — they're found through "word of mouth."

2. Keep your eyes 'n' ears peeled: Check out the daily job listings in your local newspaper and at your state job or employment service. Are "help wanted" signs posted in your community center, local grocery store, neighborhood or on a Web site? Scout them out. Is that a job your neighbor is mentioning? Look and listen wherever you go.

3. Don't be shy, just apply: You can't get a job unless you apply for it, right? Applying may be as simple as offering your services to a neighbor. Or it may involve filling out an application and talking to an employer in an interview.

    You may be asked for references — names and phone numbers of people who can vouch for your character and skills, such as a coach, family doctor or teacher. It's a good idea to line up references ahead of time.

4. Make a good first impression (it counts!): When you apply for a job, wear clean and neat clothes. (Employment experts even tell adults that!) Arrive on time or early. Be courteous and mention any skill or experience you have that is relevant to the job. But don't try to be someone you're not. Just be yourself.

How much is the "minimum wage" in your state?

By law, it's the lowest hourly wage rate an employer can pay you.

Find out at your local job or employment office.

How Much Is Payday?

It's not easy talking about money, especially when you're a kid applying for a job. A *Zillions* magazine kids' job survey reports that only about one in six kids asks what the pay is before taking a summer job! The kids said they didn't want to ask because they felt they might not get hired and they didn't want to look "pushy" or "greedy."

But the main reason kids want jobs is to make money. So it's important to find how much a job pays and exactly what you're expected to do. That way you can figure out whether or not it's worth it.

Want to Be a Millionaire?

Here's Looking at You, Inc.

So you want to be a millionaire and you're thinking of starting your own business to get there? Check out this crash course on entrepreneurship (running a business).

Find a Bright Biz Idea

Starting your own business all starts with you, so make a list of things you like to do. That way, you can make money and have fun, too. Now look at your list. What things do you do well? Of those things, what will people pay you to do?

Great business ideas are based on things people need and want that are done with a new twist. For example, if you started a business cutting grass, you could also offer the service of fertilizing and watering gardens and lawns.

You're the Boss

Being your own boss may sound like fun, but it also means making lots of decisions. For example, how much will you charge? What hours will you operate each day?

Just because you're making all these decisions doesn't mean you're the big cheese. You have to satisfy your customers, or they'll do business with someone else. So each customer is like the boss! What's more, you must make sure you follow all legal regulations and safety laws. (Ask an adult to help you check this.)

Whoa!

Bill's Billions

Does Bill Gates, founder and chairperson of computer software company Microsoft, have a secret gateway to wealth? In 2003, *Forbes* magazine estimated Bill's fortune to be worth a hefty $40.7 billion! He's the richest entrepreneur in the world.

Maybe Bill's secret was starting early. He wrote a computer program to play tic-tac-toe when he was just thirteen. When he was nineteen, he started Microsoft.

Back then, in 1975, computers were clunky machines about the size of a desk. But when Bill saw a magazine article about a computer small enough to fit on top of a desk, he thought computers would become valuable tools that no office or home could do without. He was right — today, computers are everywhere!

Casing the Competition

What's your competition? Are other kids or companies selling the same product or service in your neighborhood? How much are they charging? Find out so you can make sure your price is in the same ballpark. Otherwise, you may be charging too much or too little.

What's It Going to Cost You?

Do you need any equipment or supplies to make your product or deliver your service? How much will they cost? How does this compare to the price you're charging? You want to buy your supplies at a low price and sell your product or service for a higher price. If you don't, you'll lose money instead of make it.

Marketing Your Biz

If nobody knows about your business, there's no way anybody can buy your product or service, right? So make business cards or flyers and hand them out. Look for cheap and wacky ways to grab people's attention.

Start-Up $$$$

Do you need cash to start your business? If so, try asking your parents or someone you know well for a loan. The fact is many small businesses are started with cash from family and friends. Experts call this "love money." But don't get down on your knees and grovel for it. Write up a business plan (see below) to show them you mean business!

Writing a business plan will also help you decide how to run your business and what you need to do to make a profit. What's more, it will help you figure out how much you can afford to pay for a loan and still make money. Don't forget — money lenders usually charge a fee called interest for the use of their money (page 28). The cost of borrowing money is another cost of doing business!

Grab a pen and start writing!

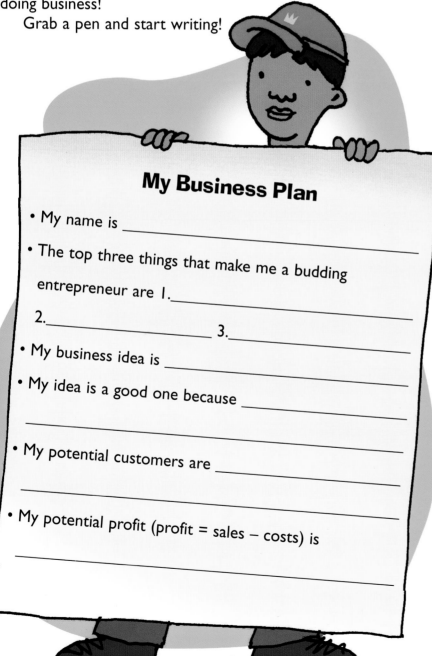

My Business Plan

- My name is _____

- The top three things that make me a budding entrepreneur are 1._____

  2._____ 3._____

- My business idea is _____

- My idea is a good one because _____

- My potential customers are _____

- My potential profit (profit = sales − costs) is _____

Lottery Odds Stink

If you think winning a lottery is your ticket to a million bucks, think again! First, you must be eighteen or older to buy a lottery ticket. Second, you're more likely to be struck by lightning than to win a lottery jackpot. While the odds of being killed by lightning are 1 chance in 30 000, the odds of winning the New York Lotto, for example, are 1 in 18 009 460.

Don't despair. If you want to be a millionaire, you can get there by starting and running a successful business or by saving and investing money. Experts say it's much easier to become a millionaire by saving and earning compound interest (see page 29) than by winning a lottery. And almost anyone can do it!

Biz Kids Who Rule

The Chocolate Farm

Could you resist melt-in-your-mouth Cows on a Stick or Pigs in the Mud? Probably not if they were made by The Chocolate Farm. According to the Farm's Chief Chocolatier Officer, Elise Macmillan, she and brother Evan have sold "tens of thousands" of these chocolates since they went into business in 1998.

Selling through stores and their Web site, the entrepreneurial whiz kids have turned handmade chocolates into big business. In 2001, the Chocolate Farm's revenues topped $1 million!

Elise learned to make chocolates from her grandmother at the age of 3. When she was 10 and Evan was 13, they wanted to have a business. "I like chocolate, Evan likes working with computers and we both like animals," says Elise. "The Chocolate Farm seemed like a great idea."

They "bought a few molds, some chocolate, made some Cows, Clouds, and Pigs in the Mud and sold out," says Elise. "Evan put up a Web site, we got more orders, and everything took off."

2 Bored Boys Inc.

When Matthew Balick and Justin Lewis were 8 years old in 1997, they invented a toy. The two boys were bored silly at a basketball pizza banquet. So they began fooling around with the three-legged stands in pizza boxes that prevent the cheese from sticking to the top.

"You can push down on the middle of a stand and then let go to make it shoot into the air," Matthew says. BOING! The next thing they knew, everybody around them was flipping the stands.

So Justin and Matthew started their own company 2 Bored Boys. Inc. and teamed up with Itz Toys to manufacture the toys. They added cool alien and animal faces to the stands, bright colors and called them "Flip-Itz." By the fall of 2001, Flip-Itz were being sold nationwide and were even selling out in some stores.

Do You Have the Right Stuff?

Do you have what it takes to be an entrepreneur? Take this quiz to find out.

1. You believe in yourself
a) No matter what
b) Most of the time
c) Some of the time

2. If you were playing truth-or-dare, you would choose
a) A dare
b) To tell the truth
c) To conveniently disappear

3. When you have a goal, you
a) Never lose sight of it until you reach it
b) Go after it unless a "road block" gets in your way
c) Get easily discouraged

4. When you play sports, you
a) Play to win
b) Play to have a good time
c) Like to play without keeping score

5. When you're trying to solve a problem, you
a) Come up with wacky ideas that work
b) Look for ideas that have worked before
c) Wait for the problem to take care of itself

When you've finished the quiz, count how many A answers you chose, B answers and C answers. See how you rate on page 56.

Money from Money

Money Goes to Work

Investing is taking some money and putting it to work for you. To do what? Make more money! You can invest your money in two ways.

Earning a Fixed Amount

You can put your money in fixed income investments — U.S. Savings Bonds, government bonds, corporate bonds or certificates of deposit (CDs). Fixed income investments pay you a fixed, or set, interest fee and guarantee to pay back all your money at a certain time.* So you can figure out exactly how much interest your money will earn and when you will get it back.

When you buy a corporate or government bond, you are loaning your money to the corporation or government with the agreement that they will pay it back plus an interest fee. A CD is a special deposit you make at a bank. You earn a set interest fee on it and get the deposit and accumulated interest when the CD matures.

According to to this, my hockey card collection's an investment. Cool!

Growing on Stocks

You can also put your money in growth investments — stocks and mutual funds. When you invest in stocks and mutual funds, you hope your money will grow and that what you buy will be worth more in the future than it is today. Then you can make money by selling your stocks and mutual funds. So this means rare and collector items can also be growth investments, for some people buy them hoping to sell them for much more than they paid one day.

A stock is a share, or piece, of a company. Say you buy stock in Nike or Sony, for example. That means you own a small piece of the company. Sound cool? Some stocks also pay you dividends — a share of the company's profits.

You can make more money investing in stocks than many other types of investments. But here's the catch: with the potential for such high reward comes high risk. Unlike fixed income investments, the amount of money you can make is not certain. In fact, you may lose some or even all of your dough!

Might lose all your dough? Whoa!

You can't get something for nothing!

---

* U.S. Savings Bonds are guaranteed by the government, but many other bonds and fixed income investments are not. The Federal Deposit Insurance Corporation usually insures CDs offered by banks.

Bears and Bulls

What does it mean when investors talk about bear markets or bull markets?

Bear market — falling stock prices of 20 per cent or more. The name comes from the old scheme of selling bearskins before the bears were caught. Sound risky? It was. But long ago, that's what "bearskin jobbers" did. They hoped that the price of bearskins would then fall, so they could buy the skins for less than they'd sold them for. Eventually, dropping stock prices were called a "bear market."

Bull market — rising stock prices. Long ago, sicking attack dogs on captive bears and bulls was a cruel but popular sport. Eventually "bull" came to mean the opposite of "bear." Some people say it was because bears fought back by swiping their paws down, while bulls retaliated by thrusting up their horns. But others say that's a myth.

Risky Business

Stock prices constantly rise and fall. If your stock goes up, your money grows. If it goes down, your money shrinks. But these gains and losses happen only on paper. You don't actually make or lose any money until you sell the stock. If you think the stock will go up again, you may want to hold on to it. On the other hand, it may slide further down. That's the way the market crumbles, er, tumbles!

Sound like risky business? It is! Take these steps to minimize the risk.

1. Do your research
The key to buying stocks or any investment is to know what you're buying — to research the company and its products before you buy. (Would you buy a bike without taking it for a spin? Not a chance! Buying stocks is no different.) Then, although anything can happen, you will have an idea of what to expect.

2. Don't put all your eggs in one basket
Don't invest all your money in one stock. Diversify, or buy a variety of stocks in different industries, or trades. While the price of one stock may tank, another may soar.

3. Give growth time
Though stock prices constantly go up and down, they generally go up over time. On average, investors who are in it for the long haul — holding stocks for fifteen years or more — see their money grow. But, of course, some stocks may not go up. That's the risk you take.

Mutual Funds

Putting your money in mutual funds is another way to buy stocks. When you buy shares in a mutual fund, your money is pooled with other investors' money. That way, you can buy a variety of stocks without putting in a lot of money. A professional manager decides what stocks to buy and sell. These features make buying mutual funds less risky than individual stocks. Still, there are no sure bets!

What's a 401(k) Anyway?

A 401(k) helps people save money for when they retire, or stop working. It's a retirement savings plan run by companies for their workers. It allows employees to invest part of their wages. People can also save for retirement through individual retirement accounts (IRAs) that invest their money in mutual funds, stocks, bonds or certificates of deposit (CDs).

Decisions, Decisions

Bonds? Stocks? Mutual funds? What's the right type of investment for you? It depends on your investment goals and your personality. Ask yourself these questions to help decide:

- What do I want my investment to do for me? Give me a safe place to park my money while it earns some income? (Think bonds.) Give me the potential to earn a lot of money? (Think stocks or mutual funds.)
- How much risk am I willing to take? Do I want to protect my money? (Think savings bonds and certificates of deposit [CDs], which guarantee your money.) Am I willing to risk losing some or all of it, with the hope of making a lot more? (Think stocks and mutual funds, which come with the greatest risk and the highest potential for reward.)
- How long do I have to invest? Do I need to use my money in a few months or years? (Think bonds, since you can take less risk.) Five years or more? (Think stocks or mutual funds — then you can take more risk.)

No Place Like the Stock Market

You can't go to the stock market — it's not a place. It's a term that describes the business of buying and selling stocks. But you *can* visit a stock exchange, such as the New York Stock Exchange on Wall Street. That's where professional stockbrokers buy and sell stocks in auctions for clients — investors like you.

When you want to buy a stock, for example, your broker says how much you want to pay for it, while another broker says how much his client wants to receive. Then they negotiate to agree on a price.

How do you find a stockbroker? With your parents' help. You must be at least 18 years old to buy and sell stock. You'll have to trade stocks through your parents until then.

Kids Play the Market

GO APE PICKING STOCKS

Experts say stock prices usually go up over time. But there are no safe bets. In fact, one newspaper includes a "wild card" stock in its annual stock-picking contest to remind people of this. One year, the wild card was chosen by a baby orangutan — it came in fifth among eight experts. Not bad for an ape! If you want to try picking stocks without losing any cash, try this activity.

You Will Need
- current stock pages from a newspaper or Web site
- pencil and paper
- paper clip

1. List five products or companies you know and like. Find out everything you can about each. Look for info on financial Web sites and in magazines and newspapers.

2. What stocks do experts recommend as good investments? To find out, check out financial Web sites, magazines and newspapers.

3. Use your findings from steps 1 and 2 to choose six stocks. Choose a "wild card" stock by dropping the paper clip on the stock pages or Web site printouts. Whichever stock the paper clip lands on is it!

4. Record the price of each stock in a chart (see below). Check each price every week and record it for three months, six months or a year. How did you do?

Kid Investor

Who: Devon Green, eleven-year-old owner and operator of a recycling business

Investment: Devon chose an "environmentally friendly" mutual fund. Mutual funds like the one Devon picked are called "socially responsible investments." They invest in companies that have good environmental records and promote animal welfare, and they avoid companies that don't.

The fund's ups and downs: "It's win-win either way," says Devon. "If it goes down, I can buy more shares with less money. When it goes up, my investment is worth more."

Stock Price	Hershey	Nike	The Gap	Sony	Microsoft	McDonalds	Kellogg's
When picked or bought	$63.52	$43.67	$15.18	$38.55	$46.44	$13.83	$31.30
Week 1							
Week 2							

Fake Money

Making It by Faking It

Some people will do anything to make money, including faking it. Counterfeiting bills is one of the oldest crimes around. In fact, a Chinese banknote from the fourteenth century carries the warning "Any counterfeiter will have his head cut off"!

Modern technology is making it easier and faster than ever for counterfeiters to crank out good-looking funny money. Now that counterfeiters can copy real bills by scanning them into a computer and printing them out, almost anybody can do it. In 2002, a thirteen-year-old in Pensacola, Alabama, was caught buying sodas with bogus bills he had faked on his computer.

Phony bills made with computers and color copiers often look real enough to fool shopkeepers. The fake bills aren't caught until they're deposited in the bank, where sensors in bill-sorting machines check for security features built into genuine bills.

Here's the rub. Banks don't reimburse shopkeepers or anybody else for counterfeit money — that would encourage people to deposit fake money to get their hands on the real thing when they withdraw it.

So when bogus money gets into the money system, everyone loses. Shopkeepers have to raise their prices to make up for the counterfeit losses, and you have to shell out more for stuff. Phony money makes everyone pay!

Counterfeit Crimes 'n' Capers

Painting by number$: In New Jersey in the late 1800s, Emanuel Ninger painted signs by day and phony bills by night. He drew $50 and $100 bills with pen and pencil, then colored them with paintbrush and ink. Emanuel wasn't caught for fifteen years, until he put a bill down on a wet bar and the ink ran! Many saloon keepers he had duped framed the bogus bills and hung them on their walls as art.

Movie money blasts off: When $1 billion of fake money made for the action movie *Rush Hour 2* was blown up on set, piles flew into the air and fluttered into the hands of ordinary people. Many spent the "windfall" without ever noticing it wasn't real. The movie money looked so genuine that the U.S. Secret Service banned the movie company from making any more.

2 ¢ WORTH

New money designs are created to include new technology or features — color-shifting ink, fluorescent threads and watermarks — that make money harder to fake. Take that, copycat!

The Bogus Test

You can help fight counterfeiting by knowing how to spot fake bills. If you think you've got a fake $5 bill on your hands, for example, compare it to a real one. Look for differences rather than similarities, because they're easier to spot, then compare the following security features. If you think the bill is phony, contact the police or Secret Service.

A familiar face?

Just whose mug is that on a $5 bill anyway? President Abraham Lincoln, who freed enslaved people while he held office during the Civil War in the 1860s. Bigwigs' heads have been stamped on money since ancient times. They work well as an anticounterfeit device because most people can easily spot defects in familiar portraits.

Details, details!

See the thin lines behind President Lincoln and the Lincoln Memorial on the back of the bill? Fine-line patterns like these often look splotchy when photocopied.

Microprint

Check out the thin lines in the borders on the bill's sides. They're not lines at all. They're words — "FIVE DOLLARS" — made of print so tiny they're almost invisible to the naked eye and extremely tough to copy.